Nature's Nuggets of Truth

A COLLECTION OF NARRATIVE POEMS

ANSWORTH HERVAN MOITT

Copyright 2019 by Answorth Hervan Moitt.

ISBN   Softcover   978-1-951469-93-1

All rights reserved. No part of this book may be reproduced or transmitted in any form or by any means, electronic or mechanical, including photocopying, recording, or by any information storage and retrieval system without express written permission from the author, except in the case of brief quotations embodied in critical reviews and certain other non-commercial uses permitted by copyright law.

Scripture taken from the Common Bible NRSV® copyright 1973 National Council of Churches of Christ in United States of America. Used by permission. All rights reserved.

For information, please write to answorthmoitt@yahoo.com
Call (786) 481-8223
Fax (305) 910-0224

Cover: Concept and design by Answorth H. M. Moitt.
Picture on cover is Hibiscus Rosa-Sinensis

Printed in the United States of America.

To order additional copies of this book, contact:
Bookwhip
1-855-339-3589
https://www.bookwhip.com

Dedication

Dedicated to all my nieces,
nephews, and their families.
You're the hope of our extended
bloodline in the years ahead.
Keep faith in God – your creator, helper
and sustainer of your future,
and you'll be just fine.

Thanks!

A word of thanks, gratitude and
heartfelt appreciation for the
initial editing by
Rhonda Williams and
Daisy Millin.

Contents

Introduction to Nature's Nuggets of Truth 1
Nature 7
Butterfly and Rose 8
Seaward Bound 10
Justice 12
The Wedding Song 13
The Bible 14
The Cost of Courage 15
What a World! 16
Instructions 18
Soul to Soul 19
Earth 20
Fruits 21
Technology 22
The Tree 24
What are People Like? 25
We follow in the footsteps of our Foreparents and Elders 27
Philosophy of Love 29
Time's End 31
Spirits for Bodies 33
Abiding Grace 35
When? 37
My Alphabet of Me 39
Welcome Boy! Welcome Girl! Welcome! 41

Will God Come Again to Earth?	43
Reparations for Me	45
Out of my Heart	47
Does God Really Love?	49
No Chains!	52
Hands	53
The Preacher	54
Reproduction	55
The Doctors	57
Blessed are the Poor	59
Money	60
Loving You	62
Using Time Wisely	63
To whom do you Pray?	64
The Offerings	65
Before the end Comes	66
May I Remind You?	67
Life's Fountain	68
Did You Know?	69
Crisis of Conscience	71
For the Children	73
Death Row's Death	75
For Janice	76
Marcelle J. Williams	77
Daisy-Mae Millin	79
Friends for Life	81
Divisions	83
Equilibrium	85
Now is the Time	87
Eulogy for Indonesia	88
Hallelujah!	90

A Christmas Wish	91
Judgment Day	93
Above or Below?	94
I'm Not Forgotten	96
The Art of the Artists	98
Open your Eyes! Open Your Heart!	100
Celebrate Life	102
Can You See?	103
Freedom	104
The Conflict	106
The 35th Miami-Dade Book Fair	108
Fire	110
What to do in Order to Love Your Neighbor?	111
What Shall I Bequeath my Child?	113
In Remembrance of You	115
What is Man?	117
What Man Needs?	119
The Vicissitudes of Life	120
My Wish for You	122
Thanksgiving	123
A Simple Solution to a Thorny Problem	125
The Perils of the Ancient Farmer	127
Lines and Voices	129
Spring into Easter	132
Falsehoods	133
Birds	134
The Church House	136
Before You Pass On	138
Emotions	139
For the High School Graduate	141
Meditations	143

Which Move?. 145
For All Mothers. 147
The Movements of Music 150
If Only. 152
The Voice 154
The Woman in the Window 156

Alphabetical Index of Topics. 159
Biography. 163

Introduction to Nature's Nuggets of Truth:
A Collection of Poems

Poetry is an international art form within the corpus of literature. Its forms are numerous due in part to its development from ancient times and places.

As early as fifteen-fifty BCE, there are some lyrical verses found in Exodus attributed to Moses with a call and refrain (Exodus 15: 1-19NRSV).

The Greeks gave Lyrical poetry to the world as early as the seventh century BCE. The first of its kind was a form of chant and response by a choir, and later, the poet stood out as an independent vocalist.

With the passing of time, other forms such as the Epic, Free Verse, Ode, Elegy, Concrete, Lists, Narrative, Pastoral and Sonnet were developed.

Each form is differentiated by structure, theme, purpose, rhyme and rhythm, line, stanza, and tone. As such, the poet can make the subject fit the chosen or desired form for greatest impact.

The subjects tackled in this volume are tinged with the religious faith of the poet's background. It is the lens though which he views the world, thus making the tone of most of the pieces optimistic at best.

The poems come from an observant eye and penned with a mind to educate; to cause the reader to stop and think, as well as to enhance discussion on the topics chosen, in order that action be taken to correct negative attitudes and dispositions that adversely affect personal, communal and environmental life.

These verses are in some small way comparable to those of Solomon the Wise, who also in his teaching method, utilized the power of observation of very mundane things, such as creepy crawlers and insects. He observed that *"Lizards and spiders are in king's palaces,"* (Proverbs 30: 28 NIV); the fly in the apothecary's ointment creates a stench (Eccles.10: 1 NIV); and, he says, *"Go to the ants and learn"* (Proverbs 26: 6 NIV). He also observed that the wise and foolish end up the same way in death since wisdom cannot save from death's power (Eccles. 2: 16 NIV).

Jesus of Nazareth was also an observer of natural things. He used His power of observation also as a teaching mechanism in order to concretize the imparted lessons of life. On one occasion, in an effort to help his listeners to understand God's eternal care, He said, *"Look at the birds of the air; they do not sow or reap or store away in barns and yet, your heavenly Father feeds them,"* (Matt. 6: 26 NIV). On another occasion, St. Mark records a parable Jesus told with the same underlying meaning of God's power to take care of people's concern (Mark 4: 26-29 NIV). The farmer's job was just to plant seed. He sleeps and wakes; sleeps and wakes over a number of months. The seed sprouts, grows, and produces the harvest – all by nature's power under God's control. The point is, God is always in control and not man. We are responsible for the small insignificant thing as putting seed in the soil and God does the rest in His time.

Now, I am not in any way equating my humble mind to that of these great teachers of old; not for a nanosecond; only to show that if one keenly observes nature, man, and the universe, much can be learned and then taught to the next generation. As teachers and elders of our communities, we are responsible to train the next generation in this skill of observation. Hopefully, these verses will enhance the reader's consciousness in like manner.

The first poem *Nature*, the second *Butterfly and Rose*, and the eleventh *World*, look at the world in all its grand design, beauty and elegance with a desire to influence the reader to take greater care to preserve it for the next generation.

The third poem *Seaward Bound* takes a realistic view of what we are doing to our pristine oceans and by extension, our waterways; by dumping garbage and sewage that is choking sea and fresh water life. Marine scientists claim that coral reefs are experiencing death at an alarming pace. Something must be done to rehabilitate our seas and waterways for future generations.

In *What a World*, the tone shifts from optimism to realistic pessimism, seeing things as they really are with little hope of change. But beneath it, is a yearning for a settlement between the Jewish and Palestinian conflict. World leaders must not just sit and wait for the inevitable destruction of the Palestinian or the Rohynga people. Now is the right time to act courageously.

Technology looks back with a tinge of nostalgia, and forward with some hope that abuses in the system would be eradicated.

What are people like? is intended for the humorous reader, but just like the Stingray, it has a point for the naive to be wary. People are not always what they appear and beneath the smiley greeting their intensions can be sometimes deadly.

St. Luke records Jesus in His instructions to the one who wanted to become His follower, said, "Count the cost,"(Luke 14: 28 NIV). *The Cost of Courage* requires that kind of evaluation; since it is not popular to *blow-the-whistle* on wrongdoing, the brave and courageous must also weigh the pros and cons before going forward. Even though it is the right moral action to take, it is not as easy and many shy away from so doing because of the heavy price that must be paid. This is a value that must be impressed upon the young so that they do not just let wrongdoing slide by the wayside or turn a blind eye to injustice.

Instructions tell of a mother's concern for her child that's bent on rebellion. Sometimes, parents have a real hard time molding a child to do what is right. Parents must compete against the peer pressure of the child's friends and acquaintances in order to keep them on the straight and narrow way.

Soul to Soul is in the voice of a devoted lover who thinks that the soul speaks much more eloquently than the body; thus, he uses his soul to communicate his mind and heart to the beloved.

Love is a major phenomenal part of human nature and experience. For most, it is an emotion that is stirred by physical attributes of the beloved. Yet, at a profound level, love is a philosophy which must be dissected to reveal its structural parts. **Ethos** and **pathos** are the foundation stones on which love is built for it to last, and when this is understood, accepted, and practiced, then love flourishes and enhances the relationship for all time. This understanding is the secret to long-lasting fraternal and marital relationships.

There are a few poems on the theme of *Time*, the commodity that humans have no direct control in that we do not know how much of it is allotted to us and when exactly it will end. The desire is for the reader to evaluate each day's activity so as to improve the future use of it.

No Chains and *Reparations for Me* are two pieces on the same theme of past slavery and present slave practices engineered to keep production high and wages low. Slavery today is more economical and psychological than physical; therefore it is vital to be wary of those companies and commercial establishments that provide no bargaining or union representation for its workers

My Alphabet of Me harks back to Jeremiah's declaration, *"Before I was conceived in my mother's womb, He knew me,"* (Jeremiah 1: 5; Psalm 139: 16-18 NRSV). Again, the poet wants to emphasize especially to the young that their being on this planet is not by happenstance, not by some act of fate in evolution, but rather through the thoughtfulness and ingenuity of a caring creator, God.

Welcome Boy! Welcome Girl! Welcome! This expresses the joy of a new addition to a family that waited for a long time for a child. There should be joy, gladness, and rejoicing over a newborn since the infant is an extension of hope in a future that all will be will for the family.

There are also five poems that raise questions on the *Coming of God to the world*.

Does God really love? Is the poet's response to the question raised by a presenter in a theological seminar; whose view says God cannot really love.

To whom do you Pray? This is recognition that other religious faiths and practices validate speaking to God about themselves and the needs of the world. It is the hope that the young will be ecumenical in their religious understanding.

Did you Know looks back at some historical facts that may not be highlighted in school curriculum today but needs to be known.

For the Children is a tribute to the children of the world with hope of liberation from slavery, child labor, harassment, physical and sexual abuse, and poverty. They are to be given every conceivable opportunity to rise in fulfilling their dreams and aspirations.

Death Row's Death came to me while listening to a sermon in church recently. I saw the process much like chained prisoners on the night of their execution; only that it was all humanity facing annihilation. But Christ has changed that death sentence to life eternal. Death will be ultimately eliminated.

Friends for Life is the opposite of *Divisions*. Divisions pit people against each other based on their ethnic, socio-economic, religious, and political differences.

Eulogy for Indonesia tells of the destruction and the hope of new beginnings for the recovery of the nation's devastation that killed so many children and adults in the latter half of 2018.

There are four family pieces that are personal to the poet; *For Janice*, celebrating our forty-first wedding anniversary. In tributes to celebrate the birthdays of two of my sisters; for *Marcelle* and *for Daisy* are dedicated. *The Art of the Artist* is dedicated to my artist niece R. I. Williams.

The other entries need no further explanation. It is the poet's hope that these verses will inspire, challenge, motivate and educate to the point of deeper discussion and action. To you, with best wishes!

Answorth H. Moitt.

Nature

Velvet rains –
penetrate the soils,
silent winds-
rock the trees; call the bees,
pollinate the blooms,
induce the seeds,
bring forth the fruits,
by the power of the radiating sunlight.

Quiet rivers,
crystal waters,
oceans in a sea of blue;
skylight bright on starry nights,
beckoning, calling me and you,
to stop and ponder,
cheer and figure;
what the Almighty hands still do.

Butterfly and Rose

(A young boy is in love with the ecology of his garden and plays imaginary question/answer games with the plants and insects).

Butterfly, butterfly,
What is your reason?
What are you in this world to do?
No reason at all I can think of,
except to display my beautiful shape
and colors; red, white, green, yellow,
black and blue.
To visit blooms and drink their nectar,
fly for thousands of miles
from north to south in fall
for winter;
molt and multiply and fly back again
for spring and summer.
That's something I'm sure
You cannot do,
that's the reason for my being here.

Miss Rose! Miss Rose!
What is your reason?
What are you here in the ground to do?
I don't know for sure?
Except to say, to produce my blooms

Of every color;
Red, white, yellow cream,
give a pleasant perfume scent;
to beautify the homes and palaces,
to be given to friends,
to lift broken spirits
sick with fear and near to death;
to bring joy and hope everywhere.
That's what I think that I'm here to do.

Seaward Bound

There was a time
not so long ago,
in nature's pristine seas;
creatures there
were uninhibited;
moved without
obstruction
across one ocean
and back again.
But today, that
lifestyle seems ended.

Seas have become
sewers,
dumpsters,
littered with human trash,
oil spills, chemicals,
plastics, toxins,
factories' wastes.
Sea creatures' lives
are in danger –
species extinction
inevitable
if nothing is done.

The time is now
right for retrieving
the garbage
from our seas;
Who will act?
Who will pay?
it must not
be left that way.
United Nation, make a plan,
involve the nations
everyone must
put a hand to clean up
the oceans.

Justice

Call it what you may,
retributive justice, poetic justice,
Law of Karma,
fate of the gods,
principle of sowing and reaping.
The good you do, comes back to you,
the evil you do comes back to you,
both in this lifetime
and the next.

Justice is said to be blind,
but often not.
For too many innocent
are unjustly judged
under the law.
The guiltless often suffer for the guilty,
while the lawbreaker runs free,
to commit other wrongs
with little consequence.
But the Great Judge will settle accounts
in His time and way.

The Wedding Song

She took my name,
she played my game,
she went along and sang my song,
she took me in,
make me feel just like a king.
That why I love her.

Chorus
I'll never let you go,
I'll never let you cry,
Except tears of joy,
For the birth of our
Boy or girl,
That's why I now say
I do to you,
And it's forever;
Till the day I die.

She is indeed a wonder,
she's brought much to
me to ponder.
That she was here,
and I was there without her.
But here we are together,
before the altar,
That's why I love her.

I know that changes will come,
and times may get
tough and hard;
but we'll fight the
storms together,
with great faith in each other,
And hope that will tie us over
the years of time.

The Bible

The bible is dialectic of faith, a conversation between God and mankind, on the themes of creation, sin, and redemption.

B – Because He lives;
I – Into my heart His grace is poured;
B – Before His throne I stand each day;
L – Loves me, He does with an everlasting love;
E – Eternity He has prepared for me.

Is there another book that influences your life?
Does it give you strength in your weakness?
Does it provide Light in your darkness?
How about wisdom in times of your folly?
Does it have a pervading living spirit?

The Cost of Courage

Apprehension, fear, distrust, frustration, all
Stand in the way of taking a courageous action
Once these are overcome, and action taken
Retribution, vilification, ostracization, and misery
Will be your portion
Yet, you must walked on the path of courage,
For your brave deed; your living, home and head maybe lost

Spouse and children, standing with your decision,
To the point of their detriment, lose their bread,
That's just part of the price to be rewarded
For courageous action, not on a field of physical battle
But right in the community instead

Medals are given to war fighting soldiers,
For courage and bravery in the battle,
Much ado is made of thanking for service,
But for the whistleblower, the courageous corrector;
Hate, scorn, and ingratitude are poured on their heads,
That's part of the price which cannot be refined

What a World!

Solace Sustains
Fixed feelings
Myriad motives
Powerless peace
Politicians' practices

Dignity devoured
Greed gratified
Indulgences un-indicted
Calmness crucified
Ethics Electrified

Underage uncommitted
Families fully frustrated
Teachers terrorized
Pastors/priests petrified
World wonders

Downfallen derided
Prosperous pampered
Vanity valued
Vices veiled
Salvation shunned

Resistance railroaded
Reparations not righted
Prisons populated
Juveniles judged
Condemned and confined

Exercise entered
Weight wasted
Meals meager
Fruits for figure
Bodylines linger

Jews un-justified
Palestinians pushed
Seward survival
Rohingyaans robbed
Homeland harassed
What a world!

Instructions

Look here! Look there!
look around you, everywhere.
Observe on your right and on your left,
watch your back, make sure you're secure.

Listen this! Don't listen that!
Stretch your mind only with the facts,
apply them regularly and you will see,
how great a person you'll turn out to be.

Come here! Go not there!
For there are dangers you may not be aware,
stand for your thoughts and defend the right,
for so doing you'll share the light.

Stand straight! Don't bend your back!
Take pride in your work,
learn to give back,
others will help to pick up the slack.

Soul to Soul

With every heartbeat of my Soul, and
with every nerve cell of my Soul, and
with every fiber of my Soul, and
with every grace of my Soul, and
with every power of my Soul, and
with all the strength of my Soul, and
with every serious thought of my Soul,
I reach out to your Soul,
Communicating my love,
Affection,
Appreciation,
Alacrity,
Altruism,
Benevolence,
Gratitude,
Honor;
So that
When we meet Soul to Soul,
We shall be known, souls touching each other.

Earth

Mountains high, lush
valleys below;
oceans blue, rivers
clear as crystal;
grasses in a pageant of greens,
making earth's beautiful,
natural scenes.

Magnificent beasts, elegant trees;
kaleidoscope of colorful rocks,
plants for food of various kinds,
making man and beasts
with insects thrive.

Sun and moon are
placed in order,
shifting day into night;
changing seasons
for our calendar,
aging everyone by their
encircling light.

Storms have come and
are still coming,
washing away the grime of earth.
Spring and summer;
fall and winter,
changes every earthy
human being.

Hurricane Florence
has left a deluge,
North Carolina submerged below,
homes, crops, industry,
and animals,
will be unrecovered by
years on years to come.

Should we then be very careful?
spending earth's resources well,
For we will be held responsible,
by coming generations
who will tell.

Fruits

Fruits are the natural foods
grown on trees,
great for fiber, vitamins all.
Full of juices sweet or tang
solid flesh with seeds,
furnishing the consumer
with nutrients and power and strength.

Have your fill of what you like;
grapes, apples, mangoes ripe,
pine, guavas, kiwis, plums;
oranges, melons, berries all,
bananas, figs, peaches, persimmons
durian, dumps, pomegranates, sapodilla,
tamarind, soursop or dragon fruit.

What about the fruits of your labor?
Are they sweet or sour?

Technology

When I was a pre-school lad
I learned to count on an abacus, bottle stoppers, and stones.
There were no calculators or automatic machines,
We learned our times tables in rote unison;
written on the black chalkboard.

When I was a lad of ten,
radio was all we had to expose us to the wider world;
it was news and broadcasts of local concerns,
and music from 6:00 AM to 9:00 PM daily,
For the community's listening pleasure.

Later on as a teenager,
Black and white television came on the scene.
With stories and lessons in morality,
endeavoring to lift our spirits from doldrums to ecstasy;
but today, computers are now everything.

Walkman and CD mobile players are consigned to
the dump-heap of technology's history;
All mobile music is now fully loaded on the
I-phone and I pod;
It's now a plugged-in generation of post millennial children.
New technology has now taken over the world.

When I was a college student,
Word processors were just replacing typewriters;
and before I was done, personal computers;
the World Wide Web, Face Book, Linked-in, and
Email were connecting people from
here to Timbuktu.

Online banking, Amazon shopping,
are now fraught with untold perils;
For your personal detailed information
are now traded on the deep dark web,
How soon will it end? Can you tell? Ring the bell!

Advancement in educational and medical technology,
are vital to our present time.
Science and culture are the big beneficiaries,
aviation and seafaring travel as well.

Drones, like grasshoppers fill the air,
Killing indiscriminately children, enemies, everywhere.
Warzones are left littered with the wreckage,
of destruction and frustration, with no hope of
Reconstruction

Three D technology can now build you a house, saving
forty percent of cost and thirty percent of time;
It can also build prosthetics
For children and adult's normal lifestyle.

The Tree

"What is a tree good for Daddy?"
Shade for one thing, for another,
it absorbs carbon dioxide and produces oxygen
to keep you and me alive.
It is the raw material for making paper;
turned into tools or musical instruments,
building construction;
toys, Russian dolls,
fire wood to keep you warm in winter.
Its bark and leaves sometimes have
medicinal value,
it may be ornamental or enhancing celebrations,
strong and protective;
produces fruit for consumption,
We give it a name to differentiate it from
others of its kind.
Spruce and Maple, Chestnut and Pine,
Cypress and Olive;
Hazel and Aspen,
Coconut and Mango,
Soursop and Lime.

What are People Like?

Some people are like Angel Fish to look at,
Sweet as potato pie and twice as nice
On a winter's night;
Pleasant, honest, loyal friend;
Gives the best effort, sources, and very kind.

Some others are like fish of the worst specimen,
Seeking always one-upmanship over time,
Swordfish with a point to make;
Piranha working in tandem to destroy the prey,
Sharks with open mouth waiting for you all day.

Yet, some others are like the Doctor Fish,
With a ready prescription for other's woes
beside their own
Prodding into details not really their concern
And yet, others are like Octopus,
squeezing
The substance out of those who enter their path;
Yet, others act like
The stingray that will kill you with its deadly dart

And there are those like the poisonous Stone Fish,
You dare not step on it by mistake,
Keep your distance from the Lion Fish;
The Green eel, the Star gazer, and Toadfish;
Predators all, they usually show up without a call.

We follow in the footsteps of our Foreparents and Elders

From the onset of human development,
Children are inculcated into the profession of their families;
In the main, daughters emulate the chores and practices of mothers,
Sons follow the trade and professions of fathers,
In essence, they do what generations of the past
Handed down to them through tradition

From the onset of human history,
humanity has been plagued by vices over virtues,
foolishness over wisdom;
hatred, greed, avarice, and malevolence over love,
moderation, generosity and benevolence.
Is it an illusion then to believe
that right will ultimately
triumph over wrong in this lifetime?
Is it?

From the onset of civil society,
politicians, governments and religion
create dependency for relief.
But instead of betterment, what do we find?
Abuse of resources; disadvantage and deception.

Where will it end? When will it end?
How many more generations must endure before it ends?
Maybe we need to ditch following the footsteps of our foreparents
And follow our intuitive consciences instead!
Get it?

Philosophy of Love

Love is a complex phenomenon
never the same through the passing of time.
On the one hand, it has at its core, *ethos* and desire
for truth, right thoughts, and actions.
On the other hand, at its center,
it has *pathos* and patience with the beloved.
Pathos is the enduring character of love,
Ethos is the justification for love,
both *ethos* and *pathos* intertwine in relationships
that will grow and glow over long periods of time.

Sometimes love enjoys moments of laughter and happiness
in personal and communal high achievements.
At other times, love experiences heartfelt sorrow over
failure to achieve goals and plans of potential.
Yet, love comforts, protects, cares deeply for the other by
whom it stands ready to lift up,
not willing to turn its back in anger or frustration.

How do we love?
Is it in our innate nature to love?
Is love an art to be perfected by few and not the rest?
Can any survive without the love of others?
If there is only a desire for *ethos* without *pathos*,
can we still refer to it as love in the relationship?

Chaos comes when *pathos* departs,
depriving harmony of love's true existence.
Making life looks like deforestation –
bare, naked, destitute of the greenery of beauty;
hopelessly dry – circumventing growth.

Time's End

Time comes to an end, for most individually,
for some, in groups through tragedy,
but not all at once for everyone.
Some come into the world without seeing its light,
others live out a day or two, a month or so,
while yet others, live for decades upon decades.
But, as for their time, it comes to an end.

Time ends not just at death for everyone,
for when the life gifted to us stops its living,
love ends, light departs, creative energy spent,
hope is encased in darkness, troubles oppressed,
joys captured by unhealthy practices,
peace gives way to anger, wrath, and chaos.
Time ends while the individual is still breathing.

Are we dead in spirit while physically alive?
Take a cursory look around,
what do we see?
Thanatos walking in the halls of fame,
halls of governments,
halls of justice, and faith societies;
gathering more at greater frequency
victims from the masses.

Through the voluntary vulnerability of our weakness,
desiring death's comfort more than the joys of living.

Prevention of premature death depends most
often on mental acuity, spiritual strength,
and careful observation
of current and historic events.
Never giving-in to the baser urges of *sarx*,
but advancing toward the higher calling of reason,
Set by the mind toward the ultimate goal – life!

Spirits for Bodies

Spirits dwell with Him on high,
waiting to indwell the ones birthed below,
by His command they enter here,
on the birth of those He chooses.

Body and spirit synchronize
becoming one personality,
integrated for existence on this sphere.
If not so, chaos ensue,
causing split personalities,
tug of war between spirit and flesh.

As in Adam, so in Eve,
and to all those who choose to believe
that they have a spirit, a soul, a gift
from God, the creator,
who calls and stores them for His time.

He does not give an old spirit to the new life,
but for the sake of accountability true,
each individual is given a new
unique spirit, guaranteed for life.

At the end of life's journey,
It must return to God who gave it
in its pristine form,
not soiled or hardened,
encrusted with sin;
but strengthened, pleasing,
glowing for Him.

Abiding Grace

The grace that holds me fast dwells not in me,
comes not from a distance to me,
but rather from God
who is closer than my jugular.
Grace, abiding grace,
sustaining grace,
grace that holds me fast
will forever last.

Without this grace there is no real mercy,
justice without grace is the fulfilling of law.
Without *pathos* the foundation of love
is to be graceless –
all detrimental to life.
Grace, abiding grace,
sustaining grace,
grace that holds,
is necessary
for you to be held fast.

Grace is greater than unrighteousness,
It overcomes it;
Grace is greater than a depraved mind,
it subdues it;

greater than ambition,
greater than political power,
greater than wealth;
grace will defeat death
and demonstrate its power
in resurrection and new life.
Grace,
abiding grace,
sustaining grace,
grace that brings
about everlasting life
will hold us fast!

When?

He says to her…

> When will you come straight and walk right with me?
> When will you change your rebellious ways and
> act the way you're supposed to toward me?
> When will you understand my affections and love
> for you will not be shared with another?
> When? Tell me straight, when?

She says to him…

> You ask me when with all your questions,
> But, when will you stand up and defend my honor?
> When will you respect my privacy and quiet hour?
> The grass is overgrown, the children undisciplined;
> When will you take responsibility?
> When will you put a hand?
> When will you give attention to chores around
> here? When? Tell me when?

Polis says to the Government…

> When will you fulfill your promises made to us last election?
> When will our children's education be improved?
> When will school leavers find jobs to support their families?

We're paying road tax and our cars are still
falling into pond-like holes in the road;
When will the cost of living come down?
When will life become manageable for the poor?
Tell us when? When? When?

Government responds to polis…

Don't be in too great a hurry for all your demands to be met,
remember, "Rome wasn't built in a day."
We have much time left in this term to get things done;
actions are in the pipeline to change education,
roads, health cost and taxes will come down,
but we cannot now exactly say, when!

My Alphabet of Me

A- Is for my Adam's apple. Arm, ankle, artery and aorta;
B- Is for my belly, bottom, brain, breasts, and bones;
C- Is for my chest, cardiovascular system and the rest;
D- Is for my dentures since I've lost most of my real teeth; my diaphragm protecting my chest organs;
E- Is for my ears and eyes open wide on both sides to hear and see the world;
F- Is for my face lifted most times to the sun in laughter, and sometimes disfigured by my tears. F is also for my feet, bony and strong enabling me to walk and run, skip and jump.
G- Is for my gut-feeling, right or wrong;
H- Is for my hands to write and work, my head, hip and hair which is now pepper and salt looking, with hormones in low supply
I- Is for my intestines large and small churning food into liquid; immune system protecting my health
J- Is for my jaw and joints with my jugular to nourish my head
K- Represents my knees, kidneys and knuckles – a new triple K;
L- Is for my lips, soft and red; lungs that keep me breathing; liver and ligament working in harmony
M- Represents my mouth, mandible, and marrow creating bones, and also my mind that directs my actions;
N- Is for my nose enlightening me with fragrances pleasant; my nerves that keep me steady and calm in anxious moments, and also my navel which reminds me that I was once attached to my mother in the womb;

O- Is for my occipital lobe
P- Is for my pelvis, pituitary gland and
phalanges, carpal and metacarpal;
Q- Represents my quadriceps found in my thighs;
R- Is for my ribs – protecting organs of the chest
and abdomen; retina; and rectum;
S- Is for my sides – left and right, shoulders, skeleton, enabling me
to stand upright and my skin, in which I am very comfortable;
T- Represents my tongue, tonsils, tear duct, throat and thighs;
U- Is for my uvula and ulna – operates like a
crane pulled by the ligaments in my arm;
V- Represents my veins, vocal cords,
W- Is for my waist, in former times narrow but
now wide; my wrinkles and wrists;
X- Represents my x chromosome;
Y- Is for my years of life on earth and the experiences
that form my self-understanding;
Z- I was once a zygote, the earliest development of my being;
Now, all of my parts were put together not haphazardly but
rather thoughtfully through the wisdom and determination
of a great Creator, blessed is He forevermore.

Welcome Boy! Welcome Girl! Welcome!

Welcome to a new world,
this first day of your personal life.
You are born into a home of love,
with caring family members
who will always cherish your
presence, All the days of your earthly life.
Welcome boy! Welcome Girl! Welcome!

You came with your gender,
Soon you will be given a name,
Suitable for who you are.
Or, named for some long passed relative
to carry on that name.
Or, even something aspirational
looking forward to what you can be.
Welcome boy! Welcome girl! Welcome!
For the first few months
you will be cuddled, fed,
washed and pampered,
And so it should be.
You will stretch, grow, begin to see
and understand your surroundings and faces.
You will experience ache, pain,
joy and excitement in the process.
Welcome boy! Welcome girl! Welcome!

Jabs will hurt you initially,
but they are protections usually
against childhood diseases that could
take you away from us prematurely.
They Help your immune system to cope
with deadly viruses,
keeping you healthy and strong.
Welcome boy! Welcome girl! Welcome!

Will God Come Again to Earth?

From home and church, from teachers and moral leaders, we are
taught to live a moral life in order to meet God at His coming.
As children we look forward in expectancy
for the day when He comes;
but years roll over; we pass on to our children to
keep the hope of God's coming alive.
Then our own hearts wilt and wither in
waiting for that return.

Is it a falsehood that God will come again to earth?
Are we waiting in vain for that high occasion
when we shall be known even as we are known?
Is there yet time to change our thinking
of going to Him where He is and not to wait for Him to come to us?
Earth may never be transformed into a new paradise;
but we can be changed, put on immortality to
occupy our place with Him where He is.

It would be wise to speak less often of God's coming again to
earth, and more often of our going to meet with Him above.
That reversal would make mankind
more hopeful, and hospitable to the neighbor;
live with honor, speak with clarity,
practice greater civility, and
uphold the law of liberty.

Because we are kept in the dark as to
when we will be called to join Him above,
We would live in accord with His
perspective in view for this time
and tomorrow's eternity.

Reparations for Me

A very long, long time ago,
when my great, great, grandfather was born,
he was enslaved.
My great, great grandparents were starved,
whipped, chained and raped.
They lived, worked and died on the
plantation of the Englishman.
The fruits of their labor sweat and tears
enriched the coffers of the master.
Never a penny was paid to them.

After my great, great grandfather had passed away,
my great grandfather took his place.
He was a slave born on the same plantation
handed down to the eldest son of the Englishman.
My great grandfather cried tears of sorrow,
worked, and sweat, without payment
for his toil from rising sun to rising moon.
Never a penny was paid to him.

My grandfather and grandmother
were also born into slavery.
By 1834, the system fell;
emancipation came without
reparation for past wrongs

against my family.
Because of slavery, my father and
mother were deprived of educational
and economic opportunity; yet, the
Englishman's household, with the aid of
An uncaring church, prospered
and reveled in the ill gotten gains of
my family's free labor.
Added up all together
makes a tidy sum.
Now is the time to right the wrong;
time to repay all sons and daughters
of our slave ancestors.

Out of my Heart

From the depths of my heart's grief,
I now cry unto Thee my God and King,
I cry for help divine to console this
aching heart of mine;
that my physical strength cannot carry.
Bring your mighty power to assuage all my fear.
Hear my plea, O Lord; give ear to my supplication
Make known to me Thy wisdom and
direction for the steps I must take to make all my
wrongs right.
To forgive and to be forgiven,
to live and allow others to live,
forgetting the past and pressing
forward to the future.
Speak the eternal word for
I am needy of the way
that leads out of darkness
into perpetual day.
Lift O God the weight of a
soul depressed,
weighted down with sin, grief,
sorrow and pain,
cup my eternal spirit into your
mighty hand;
may it not be stained with the

evil of my mistakes.
Wash it, make it new;
keep it clean for Thy glory's sake,
So that I may present
it unstained and
unsoiled back to You.
Thank You, my God and King
For keeping Your
eternal promises to me.
For You, O God,
King and comptroller of the universe,
will never leave or forsake
the penitent;
those who have humbly turned to
Your majesty for grace
sufficient for this day
and hope for a future
brighter than today;
out of the valley of the
shadow of death into
Paradise forevermore.

Does God Really Love?

Someone raised this question yesterday
in a conference I attended.
It caused quite a stir within the audience for sure.
In my mind it was a settled fact that God does,
and therefore no question should be asked about that.
Yet, the speaker insisted that it is a valid inquiry,
and with that, began to share his facts.

Love is an emotion, a passion clear and simple
which God does not have;
God is pure Mind that thinks things into being.
For God to love, He would be affected and acted
upon by passion's passion of created beings
lesser than Himself, and that would cloud
His reason for being.
Therefore, we cannot impose our
anthropomorphic view of love upon Him;
as the great Greek philosophers have shown.

And in answer, someone raised the question,
"What do you do with John 3: 16,
and 1 John 4: 16, sir?"
"I have thought about and pondered those
statements for years," he replied
And this is my response;

"We often impose our viewpoint upon God,
but doing so does not make it true in the
same way we practice it.
To say that God loves the world means
impassability, that is –
God can feel our pleasure and
respond to our pain; affected by our love
as well as our hate."

That raised for me a new set of questions:
about prayer, about worship,
about God's fidelity,
about the nature of my existence.
If God can make one person rotten rich
and another live out his or her existence
in abject poverty;
Then the same God can send
torrential rains and or drought;
thinks it into being
And without feeling
pleasure or pain;
a defenseless people is destroyed.
Don't you then think
something is dreadfully
wrong with this concept of God?
Don't you think that
this idea of God is no
different than that
of the Olympian gods?

Sixty-six authorized biblical
texts all speak of God as a
concerned,
compassionate,
caring and affected by
His creation.
God is not devoid of the
Twin's *ethos* and *pathos;*
character and justification
foundation stones of the love
Relationship
between God and his creation.
God though immutable,
can be acted upon in the same way
a mother is by her
sons and daughters without
essentially changing her status.

No Chains!

Freedom's restrictions are everywhere.
People's rights are being taken away,
chaining their thoughts, minds, and bodies;
depriving them of liberal sway.
But a day is looming on the horizon
when all shall rise up and say,
"No chains for my head; no chains for my hands;
No chains for my neck; no chains for my mind."

My mind is not for propaganda chaining
or for political manacles.
It is for use of greater purpose;
of art and science, humanities and truth.
So, take the cuffs off my intelligence,
and let my mind grow strong and free;
for only then I will achieve potential,
to set the rest of humanity free.

My head will not be used as advert,
for Nike or Adidas ware.
My hands are not for your chained labor
in sweat shops you have engineered;
But to fervently work for the fulfillment
of the dreams my mind holds dear.
Your chains have become useless, even here.
No Chains! No Cuffs! No manacles! No Shackles!

Hands

Hands to hold my shopping,
hands to carry my load,
hands that clean the rest of my body,
hands to cuddle, caress,
care and comfort another soul.

Hands to stretch across to my neighbor,
giving gifts to maintain life,
hands that stop the tears from flowing,
calming those who are in strife.

Hands that write a note of thanks,
appreciating others help,
hands to guide the infant brother, sister,
helping them on the path of life.

When I've used my hands to help out others,
then I lift them high in praise to God,
or clasp them gently in prayer at worship,
hoping to continue while on this sod.

The Preacher

The Lord instructed me to say to you,
that people are fast passing away every day;
no matter how or where; take care,
we're to be prepared to meet him in the air.

The Lord inspired me to tell you'll,
it's time to heed the call of life eternal,
read the scriptures everyday;
for only so you'll know His way.

In the Bible we'll find
the mind of God for all mankind,
to guide us in the way of right,
that leads to truth and perpetual light.

Stay not back and walk in darkness,
for that path leads to separation,
that is not the way to go;
trust the Bible, it tells us so.

Reproduction

It's in our nature to multiply, reproduce,
have young ones;
in order to secure the continuance
of our social order.
But recently that growth is slowed
by those who wish
to delay, deny, delimit or even
oppose the process of addition.

Some replace a child with a cat, dog,
or some other furry creature,
finding pleasure in training,
maintaining, even introducing it by name;
refuse to abide by the Creator's order:
"Be fruitful and multiply;
and replenish the earth," (Gen. 1:28).
The affluent seems to have less
progeny, while
the poor seem to have more to
secure their lineage.
There is no designated number
that is ideal for all races in all places,
Just the ones they can support and adore.

So what will it be for you and your lover?
Will it be a life that's shared
with sons and daughters?
Will it be a life of giving, influencing?
sharing, training, keeping?
In order for humanity's future balance maintaining?

The Doctors

The doctor looks into your eyes,
shines a light into your mouth and ears,
checks your heart with a stethoscope,
analyzes your labs,
and with little expression
asks,
"How are you coping today?"

The dentist looks keenly at your teeth,
pokes each for signs of cavity,
takes an x-ray of your mouth,
examines the state of your gums,
and enquires,
"What is bothering you today?"

The cardiologist told me that I'm not fine,
my heart rate was very much lagging behind,
my arteries were not in the best of shape either,
clogged and blocked feet at a time,
surgery was needed to make things better.

"How is your vision?"
The ophthalmologist asks,
viewing my chart intensely with a smile,

your glaucoma, astigmatism will not last,
wearing these spectacles will correct the defect,
along with these pills your vision corrects.

"What's on your mind?"
The psychologist enquires,
"are you still enfolded by the quagmire?
Since your last visit, is everything fine?
Are you still dreaming of falling behind?
Have you found peace and release from your dread?"

Without the docs we would be at a
disadvantage for sure,
muddling through with our ill health
And no mental cure.
We must pray for them each night and day,
trusting that their medical wisdom
and knowledge will hold sway,
bringing cure and renewal of health
to those who are near or far away.

Blessed are the Poor

The poor are mostly blessed with contentment,
having little of this world's goods,
possessions, power or prestige.
They stand as a bulwark of God's
providence and grace.

The poor are mostly blessed with great hope -
that the future will be made better for their
children's education and social standing;
By the intervention of the
God they serve.

The poor are mostly blessed with conscience true,
striving for fairness, integrity, honesty, veracity;
pointing out society's inconsistencies of value,
in an effort to bring about greater equity,
justice and truth's mastery.

The poor are mostly blessed with fidelity,
giving out of their pecuniary or meager subsistence;
keeping covenant with the Master of the universe;
pouring all their hopes and dreams into Him
who holds their future in His Hands.

Money

No amount of money may make you rich;
neither the lack of it may make you poor.
It is a necessary living currency,
used worldwide for trade
and exchange diplomacy.

Money is also a social value system
for investment, deals, vehicles, houses,
land or oil, technology and animal husbandry;
work compensation or gifts to family.

Some will toil all their lives until death,
without amassing a thousand dollars in currency.
Yet, their lives are blessed with contentment,
sharing what they have without resentment.

Others may have an abundance of cash,
billions and trillions stashed away in gold and silver,
diamonds and pearls kept in secret, hidden away,
under false pretenses of a rainy day.

If money is gained by deception, oppression, or predatory practices,
theft of another's time, property or labor,
Paying a dollar when ten is minimal;
Then the gain is immoral, corrupt filthy lucre.

Money is an object without morality,
it is the owner that determines its moral value;
good or bad does not matter to currency,
gaining the world and loosing the soul
is the immortal fidelity.

Loving You

Elizabeth Barrett Browning, the romanticist,
penned the line, *"How do I love thee, let me count the ways."*
But let me show you why I love you in practical or realistic ways;
I love you because you are my joy, my desire, my heaven on earth;
I love you for your skills in cooking, cleaning as we work together,
To build a family with sons and daughters,
Training, instructing, growing, guarding,
And protecting against
The forces of nature with danger bent on severing the joys of love;
After forty years together; I love you more than ever
Knowing that in another four decades or so
I'll try to let you know that my love will grow even stronger,
Ethical and not ethereal or insubstantial,
But real as winter follows autumn, summer and spring,
Loving you is my reason for being.

Using Time Wisely

How one minute or an hour is spent,
May determine and signify the value of a day,
What you accomplish in a week,
May also designate the value of a month;
As goes the month, so does the value of a year.

A year passes quickly when you're busy,
It rolls over into five, ten, forty or fifty;
You may do most things routinely, habitually,
Go to the same places casually or frequently,
While time rolls on.

On reflection, we wish to change customs,
Use time more wisely with friends or family;
Oh! How we wish we could days and years recall,
Speak less, listen more, and lend a better hand;
Disallow the negatives and focus more on the positives of life.

Even if your life reaches ninety-five or
a hundred and five,
That's a short lifespan compared to time;
For it does not come to an end for all,
It continues for centuries and millennia,
And will roll along right into Christ's eternity.

To whom do you Pray?

Prayer is offered to many gods in different cultures,
In Hinduism they call on Shiva, Kali, and Vishnu;
In Islam, they call on Mohammed and Allah to the rescue;
In Judaism they cry to YHWEH to bring redemption,
In Christianity they call on Christ, the Way.

With Buddhism, Buddha gets devotion and offerings;
In Sikhism, they call on One Immortal Being,
Repeating the name (Waheguru) –Wondrous Destroyer of darkness
The abstract god that brings enlightenment,
Pure mind and reason, accessed through meditation and not strife.

What mostly do people ask of their gods?
Some ask for themselves and family and friends;
For guidance, protection, wisdom and peace,
Others ask for wealth and health without concern for others plight;
Yet, still others leave their concerns to dedicate
their requests for a world in need of love,
harmony and peace.

So when you arise today, be it early or late,
Call on your God to enhance your faith;
Give God the praises due to the name you always knew,
Be true to the calling that is precious for you;
For that God is never deaf or blind,
and will always answer you.

The Offerings

YHWEH gives creation and life,
Abraham gave his son Isaac,
Moses gave the law and commandments;
King David gave materials of gold, silver and timber,
Solomon gave the temple and wisdom;
Esther gave commitment,
Jonathan Maccabaeus gave his life.
The Greeks gave philosophy.
Mary gave her body,
Christ gives salvation, redemption, and hope;
The disciples of Christ gave the Gospels,
Paul gave the Epistles,
The early martyrs gave the witness,
Missionaries over the centuries gave themselves to foreign cultures;
Dante Alleghany gave the Divine Comedy,
The period of enlightenment gave art, science and technology,
Handel gave Oratorios including the Messiah;
Doctors today give healing,
Preachers and pastors give sermons,
Congregations give time, money and service;
Now, what will you give to elevate your God in this world?

Before the end Comes

Before the end comes, live!
Live life to the fullest extent,
Extend a hand of help and healing,
Heal the hurts of those in need with deeds and words;
Words used must lift up, affirm, strengthen, encourage;
Encourage the vulnerable; let them fill you with joy and excitement,
Excite your neighborhood through your generosity,
Generosity practiced will come back to your life;
Life then will be filled to its extent.

May I Remind You?

May I remind you that you are now a citizen here
With civic responsibilities to share;
May I remind you that you get back what you sow?
And that what goes around comes back around to you?
May I remind you also, that today's gift of time is very special?
Use it well, make it count.

May I remind you as well that actions speak louder than empty words?
Make your words match your actions,
bringing hope to all you encounter.
May I remind you that tomorrow is not promised to anyone,
So do all the good you can,
to as many as you can, with all the resources at your disposal;
Such as love, compassion, gratitude, generosity and grace.

Finally, may I remind you that when it's time to leave
This house of clay,
You and I shall not forever pass away,
But we will be changed by our deeds into eternity's day.

Life's Fountain

Many human inventions claim this title,
Elixirs' of various kinds have come and gone;
Proposed to have had renewal of youthful power and vigor,
Yet, the body's strength weakens. Skin wrinkles,
And cosmetic surgery fails.

Scripture reminds us that this physical body
is made of dust of the earth,
It perishes and is subject to destruction,
But the inner man is renewed day-by-day,
Through the grace, love, mercy of the Creator.

The true fountain of life then,
Is not in a cream or a bottle of expensive oil
of any kind; not even in a fountain of water far away;
But rather, in the mind that is stayed
and steeped in knowing God's
ways for your life.

Did You Know?

Did you know that a first class stamp
had cost 6¢ in 1970?
Today, 2019, that same stamp costs .55¢;
Did you know that in 1969,
Neil Armstrong walked on the moon
and the Concord made its maiden flight?
Did you know that the State of Israel
was born in 1948?
And today, it is one of the most advanced
countries in the Middle East?

Did you know that Jim Jones, a religious fanatic,
Killed 909 people in Guyana 1978?
And Prime Minster Maurice Bishop of Grenada
was overthrown in 1983 by the
American invading forces?
Did you know that Simon and Garfunkel's concert
at Central park was free for half-a-million
people in 1982?
"It was a time for confidences,"

Did you know that President Roosevelt in 1935
Started Social Security Administration?
Did you know that Russian Premier Nikita Khrushchev,

In 1956 said of American's, "You Americans are so gullible;
We'll weaken your economy until one day you will
Finally wake up and find that you have communism?"
Will medical insurance be socialized in 2020 to catch
up with the rest of the industrialized world?

Crisis of Conscience

In readiness for a crisis of conscience, the mind, body, and spirit go through a series of uproar, convulsions, disquiet, and uneasiness. A simple thing as, "I dare you to do whatever…" can bring on such a crisis.

In a personal crisis of conscience,
the entire body is in uproar;
the mind goes blank,
the spirit becomes disturbed,
heart rate becomes elevated,
and the body goes into temporary shock;
in order to make a choice or
right decision in the moment.

In a personal crisis of conscience,
time passes unconsciously.
all of one's energies are laser focused,
for not making the wrong decision;
the mind becomes clearer,
the spirit reconnects,
the heart rate normalizes,
because a decision is reached
and the crisis is resolved.

So when you are challenged
by a boy, a girl, or some situation
that demands a decision;
there are times to just relax, and say,
"I'll sleep on it, can't decide right away;
my mind will not permit it,
my spirit will not corporate,
my soul does not give me the green light,
neither my heart is in it,
and my body cannot take the shock
to decide on it at this time."
Then you walk away!

For the Children

For the children of my father's children!
Blessed are you to carry his illustrious name;
make him worthy of your prestige and honor,
by your reputation, duty, work and fame;
don't soil his memory by word or degrading action,
elevate yourself in society and do not humiliate his integrity.

To the children of my nation's children!
Your futures' door is now open wide;
step right in with bold confidence,
for now is the time to walk with pride.
Do your duty; turn not back, a great time to
Pick up the slack.

For the children of my church's children!
The torch of righteousness is handed on to you,
keep it burning bright within you,
so that others may see your ligh.;
Draw them to your Master's cause for right,
Keep it burning bright both day and night.

To the children of my alien nation's children!
never fight for an unreasonable cause;
Be thoughtful and rational in serving your nation,

With purpose, joy, integrity, care and honor.
Be not frenzied by others' emotions,
Live in peace and be guided by caution.

When all the children of this world's children,
are given rightful opportunity;
to dream their dreams and live their visions,
in a world where they are truly free;
then they'll know that God is with them,
guiding every step they take,
only then can leaders respect their own efforts,
for peace, tranquility prosperity, and harmony.

Death Row's Death

Death row's death
will come tomorrow,
just not today.
There are too many
on the row here;
but the law will
be changed,
amended, that's certain,
but just not today.
Death row's death
will be condemned and cancelled,
just not today;
Death row's death
will be eradicated,
just not today.

For Janice

41 roses,
41 kisses,
41 candles on a cake;
41 friends,
catered,
invited;
41 cheers
toasted,
and accepted.

41 years of trust,
41 years of joys repeated;
41 years of work
together completed,
41 years of love
given, received,
41 years of troubles
forgiven and forgotten.

41 years of memories
created,
41 periods
of forsaking,
sacrificing,
making ends meet;
41 times
of aching, chafing,
scraping through
financially;
41 years of
confidences in Him.

41st Anniversary
celebrates
your tolerance,
a feather in
your cap of grace;
your fortitude,
temperance,
giving,
caring,
making home a vivant place.
Happy Anniversary
my dear Janice!

Marcelle J. Williams

Julie, your b'day comes around
once each year like all others do.
But it's special and unique each time
because of advancing age.
Happy birthday!

You've had many b'day celebrations
marking highpoints in your life;
sixteen, twenty-one, thirty, forty, and fifty.
But this is the penultimate preceding your 70th year.
Happy birthday!

Julie, over the years, you've been a loving,
caring sister to me and my family.
We now say again, "Thank You,"
for all your care and concern.
Happy birthday!

We wish you God's kindest,
gracious blessing in your
health and finances.
But most of all, we wish for you
abundant joy and happiness in your family.
Happy birthday!

Now that you have reached advance
years to retire,
may your days be filled with
relaxation and leisure.
Don't forget to slow down,
put up your feet and chill.
Happy birthday!

Marcelle, you've never eaten the bread of
idleness nor drank the wine of laziness;
You've always been industrious,
hard working and intuitive.
That's why you'll be called 'Blessed."
Happy birthday!

From your earliest youth,
I have known you to be self-sacrificing,
self-denying, and unselfish, in your life and philosophy;
living for others, especially toward the elderly. Dear sister,
Happy Birthday!

Daisy-Mae Millin

Your name likens you to the flower Daisies,
bright, beautiful, strong and fragrant.
You bring love, hope, joy, peace and friendship
to all in your sphere of influence.
Be blessed on your birthday!

Your challenges are not different to others,
and you have faced them head-on
with fortitude, strength, determination,
courage, honor and foresight.
Be blessed on your birthday!

Daisy, you have given yourself to study
long and hard in your chosen field.
You've struggled up-hill in your clime to success.
Stay on the path until you've reached your goal.
Be blessed on your birthday!

Daisy, you've been a terrific and gracious sister,
thoughtful, compassionate and giving of your
time and resources. Thus, God's blessing will
supply your needs.
Be blessed on your birthday!

In a few short years you will reach the
Pinnacle of life.
The glorious radiance of the heavens
will shine upon you as the sun on
a field of Daisies.
Daisy, in these latter advancing years,
may the Spirit of love, beauty and light
walk with you in your pleasure, plans,
and projections; to prosper and protect you.
Be blessed on your birthday!

Friends for Life

From the very first day you made entry into my life,
You have stood with me through thick and thin Experiences;
You have counseled me, consoled me,
caused me to reflect differently on matters
and issues of the deeper life;
You have shed light on the way to a better existence;
you really cared for me and
That's why I am your friend for life.

You have brought to me joys and delights
previously unknown;
In periods of trouble, darkness and frustration;
When my creative powers were depleted,
You motivated, encouraged, inspired me to
get up, fight on, keep going,
So helpful to me you were in those days
That's why I am your friend for life.

When I was sick and
Needed comfort and help,
You came with words, balm for my spirit;
Cared for my soul, ointment for my head,

You washed my feet, took care of my fever;
Proving that a friend sticks closer than a sister;
Took me to the physicians,
Paid my medical bills until I was better;
Brought me food, sustained my life,
That's why I'll be forever your friend for life.

Divisions

From ancient times, divisions existed,
Words were invented to make the dividing line;
Then, religion, social and political entities,
Divided people of every clime.

Those who are rich loathe the poor,
oppress, oppose, control, even enslave them;
They enrich themselves off the poor's labor
Keeping them silent forevermore.

The wise say those who have not the skill
are fools to be disregarded, pay no heed;
It's a club for likeminded souls to thrill
All outsiders are destined for down the hill.

Sinners are condemned and looked down
upon by those who claim that they are righteous,
as if God had appointed them to determine
who will access His grace.

Big nations trample on the smaller ones,
Smarting them out of vital resources;
Jews often despise Gentiles
Democrats and Republicans likewise the same.

Should there be these divisions, really?
Dividing all humanity?
Like ebony and ivory,
We need each other to make the music of life,

The USA has need of all migrants
For science, education, military use;
For expanding a slacking older population
To enhance its future youthful power.

Equilibrium

Between the ears balance is maintained,
causing you to stand upright,
sit up straight,
walk erect,
run without falling.
Balance is maintained between the ears.

Between the poles the world turns,
rotates, gyrates ever so quickly;
swings right to left,
turns day into night, changing
seasons.
Balance is maintained,
The world has equilibrium.

She sees him, loves him,
honors him, works with him.
He adores her, he protects her,
He provides for her and shelters her.
They have equilibrium,
balance is maintained.

They fight all night,
they quarrel all day,
they rile each other;
they stop praying together,
their peace is gone,
their balance is off,
their equilibrium is broken,
They have no balance.

Now is the Time

Now is not the time to be physical,
but rather rational, logical and vocal.
The world is critically in need of normal,
otherwise it will be detrimental to our survival.
Every issue has now become electrical or digital,
displacing the mythical view of the universe.
It is now abnormal to be pastoral,
since some priests and pastors are sensual and sexual predators.
Now is the time to live ethically.

Eulogy for Indonesia

I grieve for you,
I cry over you;
I mourn your loss,
Sulawesi island,
Palu in particular,
There will never be
Another Friday
As dark as your disaster
In September
of 2018.
Oh Palu!
Oh, Sulawesi Island!
I mourn your destruction,
Tsunami, tsunami,
Look at what you've done?

Beautiful sandy beaches gone,
Children and youth's prospects dead;
Raging angry waves covered their heads
Unprepared, unexpected,
All unaware of the destruction.
People of Indonesia fell prey
On that earthquake day
Without a prayer, said
Oh Palu!

Oh, Sulawesi Island!
I mourn your destruction,
Tsunami, tsunami,
Look at what you've done?

You will rise again someday,
For hope will never pass away,
Those who are left will be revived
In order to keep the memory of your
Dead alive;
They are not lost in vain,
They surely will come again,
Beauty and strength will be your lot.
Oh Palu!
Oh, Sulawesi Island!
I mourn your destruction.
Tsunami, tsunami,
Look at what you've done?

Hallelujah!

Angels bending, good news bringing, *Hallelujah!*
Christ child coming, a new day is dawning - *Hallelujah!*
God in man is now residing – *Hallelujah!*

Shepherds' watching, Bright star leading – *Hallelujah!*
Magi unto Bethlehem going – *Hallelujah!*
To see Christ child sleeping, Mary watching – *Hallelujah!*

Herod is quaking, Demons stirring – *Hallelujah!*
Satan trembling while angels singing – *Hallelujah!*
Mankind is being redeemed from sin and suffering – *Hallelujah!*

Peace receiving, grace distributing – *Hallelujah!*
Death retreating, life extending for one and all– *Hallelujah!*
Eternity's power is now prevailing – *Hallelujah!*

A Christmas Wish

A chill is in the air,
whistles, bells, and pretty things
are everywhere;
additional light adorn
homes, shops, and malls;
spruce and pine tress
are dressed up,
People stop and chat
with pleasure,
a spirit of goodwill
pervades the atmosphere,
joys abound,
love is shown,
I wish this to be so
all the year round,
not just at Christmas.

Friends gather,
time seems not
to matter,
carols are heard
miles around.
Children are excited,
poems are recited,
of a Christ child come to earth

to bring salvation
hope and regeneration,
affirming that
God is with us,
God is for us,
Sin and death
Will be no more.
I wish this to be so
all the year round,
not just at Christmas.

Worship is attended
in greater numbers,
sermons are presented
with superior joy,
hope revived
in hearts that hated,
brother, sister,
father, friend.
Goodwill extended,
beggars invited,
table fellowship
comes at the end.
I wish this to be so
All the year round,
not just at Christmas.

Judgment Day

Judgment Day is on its way,
Drawing nearer every passing day;
Coming closer, gathering power,
Taking notes of all I do and say.
Judgment Day will not stay away,
Nothing will be able to keep it at bay;
Condemnation will not be the only option,
Praise and welcome can be my portion.

All with gather at the *Bema*,
To receive the verdict from the Master;
None shall lose their rightful place,
For "all well done," is by His grace.
Tears of joy and tears of sorrow,
Will be shed upon that day;
But no tears shall be on the morrow,
Of that great and final Judgment Day.
Hope to see you at the table,
With all the saints both old and new;
Works of righteousness will be recompensed,
In white robes that He will endow.

Above or Below?

If at the end of life
These two places
Turn out to be real;
And you had to choose
In which to spend eternity,
Which would you chose?

To make your choice
Information on both
is necessary;
One is above, full of light,
The other below, full of darkness;
Which would you chose?

The one above has music,
Joyous celebration,
Confirmation of one's dedication,
And the King is there;
The one below, none of these things,
Which would you chose?

In the one below
Memory lingers,
The fire of regret burns
strongest of

missed opportunities;
In the one above
No memory,
Which would you chose?
In both places
Time does not matter,
Neither will there be
transfer from one
To the other;
As one leaves here
to get to there;
So shall they be forever,
Which would you chose?

All may confess
openly that above is better,
No choice at all
Between the two;
But lifestyle really
determines the preference.
How you live
will decide for you.

I'm Not Forgotten

The One who made
Boulders and beryl,
Garnet and granite,
Goose and grasshoppers,
Takes a keen interest
In what becomes of me.

The One who made
The foxes and the fowls;
The figs and flowers
The fur and the maple,
Knows each step I take;
He leads me gently on the way.

The One who made
Waters and rivers,
Streams and brooks;
Wipes my tears when I cry;
Knows my sadness
And cheers me up.

The one who provides
Bread from heaven,
Water from a rock,

Gave sight to the blind,
Will heal my diseases
And satisfy my needs.

The One who made
The butterflies and bees,
The blooms on the trees,
The lilies of the fields;
Does know who you are
And will carry you through.

The One who created
earth and sky,
time and space,
the human race;
will keep promises made;
to everyone who has faith.

The Art of the Artists

The painter goes to the village
with canvas, paint, brush and easel,
to paint a picture of life there.
Its farms, cottages, trees and flowers,
rivers, pastures with animals grazing,
and the people with their starry nights, on canvas.

The artist goes to the seaside
to capture the life lived there.
The boats, nets, fishermen's gear,
cargo ship and cruise vessels passing;
The rocks and waves, birds flying by,
And even the whales captured in dance, on canvas.

The artist goes into the big city,
viewing buildings as high as the heavens.
And paints the aspiration of men,
their thoughts, actions, communal spirit,
Co-operation – culminating in the spire
of a cathedral, on canvas.

On my small island of birth,
Another artist was born in the 80s.
She was gifted, trained, studied the form
to hone her craft on canvas.

R. I. Williams is making her mark by
teaching school children and painting
sceneries of the island's beauty, on canvas.

The artist sits in the studio
looking deep within the self.
Paints pictures of abstracts ideas
conjured up by the mind.
Lines, circles, squares, unknown shapes
of different sizes with pigmentations rare, on canvas.

The artist is in love with the body,
the natural form of woman.
He gets a model, paints a picture,
of the head, face, hands, torso and feet.
He paints in a realistic fashion
that draws in the viewer, on canvas.

In ages past, some artists were
sponsored by wealthy benefactors,
while others were self-supported.
Some were very eccentric with
idiosyncrasies galore,
but they were all genuine at the core, on canvas.
So when you look at a painter's picture,
try and see beyond the art of the particular artist.
The hopes, aspirations, love, misery and beauty
from the mind to the heart of the painter.
In tints, variant hues, authentic and true, on canvas.

Open your Eyes! Open Your Heart!

Bread does not multiply
all by itself after baking;
it takes a wonderful
miraculous power to do that.
Water cannot become wine
all by itself,
it takes a wonderful
miraculous power to do that.
Physical hunger, thirst
and embarrassing
Situations do not all change
by themselves;
it takes a wonderful
miraculous power to do that.
Your will power, concern,
and care with your
resources will do that.

In days of old,
manna and quail
rained from heaven
to feed a hungry
liberated people.
Water flowed out of a rock
that followed them

half way in a treacherous
parched desert.
From that time to now,
God's people are still
travelling in caravans
by land and sea;
seeking that Promised Land
Of hope for a better
life with greater opportunity,
to fulfill potentiality.
Should they be turned back?
Should they be stopped?
Should they be drowned in the sea?
Open your eyes! Open your hearts!
Open your land!

Celebrate Life

Celebrate your successes,
Celebrate your experiences, small and great;
Celebrate your failures,
And learn from them;
Then set them aside,
Never dwell thereon,
Celebrate your purpose and your passions;
Celebrate your confidence,
Promote your values;
Celebrate your health
Good or ill, it will make
You a greater rounded personality;
Celebrate your friendships
And your family,
Extend your love
Beyond personal boundaries;
Find the joy that lies beneath sorrow and sadness,
Find faith that will elevate and change
Your impossibilities into realities;
Celebrate your labor, your leisure,
Your resilience, your character,
For you were created to rejoice!

Can You See?

Can you see the path ahead?
The path that gets you to your destination?
Is it a straightforward and smooth way?
Can you see clearly to find the path?

Can you hear precisely the direction?
Given to find the approach to success?
Is there competing or distracting information,
Taking your attention away?
Be sure to focus unilaterally,
On the truth that leads to the way.

Are you conscious of your
actions on the road ahead?
Are they helping or hurting your progress?
What you actually do demonstrate
your inner desires
In finding the highway
That leads to success.

Now that you've found success,
What influence have you shared with others?
Have you left directions for others to follow?
Or, have you placed more obstacles in the way?
True success enables others
To succeed on the way.

Freedom

The African-American,
And the peoples of the Caribbean,
Would be still bound up
In terrible, inhumane slavery;
But for the fight for freedom.

The fight for freedom
Still continues,
because total freedom
is yet to be won,
Freedom comes at a very high cost.

The fight for freedom
Undaunted must be;
For all humanity to be freed
Where 'ere they be,
For none should be bound eternally.

Freedom's values must be cherished
Hard won efforts through fights won;
Courage, honor, strength of character,
Shall ever be the triumph's song,
Keeping every home and hearth secure.

Do not renege on your part in the efforts,
To fight for the right of freedom's cause;
To speak the truth, to elect, to worship,
To be unrestricted, to believe,
That God sets us at liberty.

The Conflict

In the annals of human history,
A conflict arose in the highest heaven;
Between the omnipotent, benevolent God
And Lucifer – Son of the morning star;
Who challenged the authority of
Jehovah, his maker!

Lucifer had his supporters,
they sided with him for the benefits
that they would receive,
were he able to dethrone
the Omnipresent, Omniscient Yahweh
in the heavenly struggle.
A fight ensued as the conflict raged on.
Time did not matter,
seems like earth's very existence
weighed in the balance of the outcome;
and God did not have the advantage.
Lucifer and his throng fought the Creator
who appeared to give to Lucifer every opportunity,
to change, reverse, or repent.
But pride was also at stake;
and the son of the morning star refused,
for by backing down, would lose face.

Thus it came to an end in heaven,
God empowered Michael the Archangel
to smite Lucifer and cast him out
with his throng;
And thus, he landed on earth.

Here, the conflict rages on in earth,
in the minds and hearts of men;
from the time Lucifer landed here,
he staked his claim to this realm:
influencing, corrupting,
drawing humanity away from God.
Someone coined the phrase,
"It's the Devil who made me do it,"
Perhaps in an effort to abdicate responsibility;
But they are conceivably right
in view of Lucifer's power of persuasion,
for he is the master deceiver.

But there is a time in the future coming,
where Lucifer and his companions
will experience the final
wrath of Christ – the light of the world.
Doomed and confined
to eternal damnation forever.

The 35th Miami-Dade Book Fair

The book fair
was on Friday,
and I attended
with my book.
In Writers Row
I was situated
with high hopes
of parting with
many copies of my autobiography.

There were others
Like me standing or sitting
At their stations calling buyers.
Some with signs
advertising their work,
Pipe and Pulpit,
The Adventures of
Sherrie and Chubby,
by new authors on Writers Row.

The day was long
and it was cold,
with the Omni train passing
overhead every ten minutes.

Yet, the conversations
Were heart-warming
With those who stopped by
To preview my work.

There were book collectors,
Bulk book distributors;
Book technologists,
Book give-a-ways,
Book writers' interviews,
Book critics,
And none in attendance
Could escape the challenge of reading.
All in all, it was
a wonderful experience,
to have had the familiarity
and association with other writers
in one place;
with a huge variety of topics,
Subjects and ideas.
For children and adults,
Secular and religious.
It was a time of
Challenge and change.

Fire

The fire of love is excellent,
and the warmth of affection is great;
but the fire of hate burns strong
in the hearts of those without love.

The fire of ignorance burns bright,
unswerving and pervasive in the land;
but the fire of knowledge and wisdom,
Is slowly being extinguished by clans.

The fire of trust needs kindling
To be strengthened and practiced by all;
and the fire of distrust will be dampened,
eradicated from home, hearth, and shore.

The fire of courage requires stirring
In the hearts of the young today,
Weaning them off narcotics fire;
So that cowardice will not win the day.
What burns in your heart today?

What to do in Order to Love Your Neighbor?

In order to love
thy neighbor,
you need to be in a state
of patience; have a great attitude,
not easily aggrieved.
Not being hostile
to new views of
old concepts.

In order to love
your neighbor,
You must be tolerant
of errors,
forgiving of misdeeds,
cheerful when angered,
hold counsel when
not asked;
Strong – emotionally, mentally, and physically
when the other is weak.

In order to love
thy neighbor,
you may have to
give up some rights,
give space for
growth, gather new data,
grieve for the loss
of old ideas that are
being relinquished;
and the new ones embraced.

In order to love
thy neighbor as thyself,
Don't take yourself too seriously,
be gracious with your time,
be kind with your words,
be, thoughtful and considerate with actions;
Hold yourself to integrity,
be a true confidant to the other;
in this you will be a friend.

What Shall I Bequeath my Child?

What must I leave
my child, the love of my life?
Some land? My business investments?
Houses and cars?
Much money?
Must I leave to my child
the copyrights to my intellectual property?

My child may need all of the above and more,
But those material things are not as
Important as character,
Footsteps for my child to follow.

Material things can be squandered,
wasted and depleted over the passing of time;
Learning vicariously from others' example,
material things must be
accompanied by sound character.

It may be to my child's benefit and advantage
for me to leave a good reputation,
Moral rectitude, honor, integrity, courage,
And a reputation for decency, honesty, compassion,
friendship, respect and service.

For my child to inherit my value system,
these traits I must start to demonstrate
now that my child is two days old;
So that my child will inculcate
my moral values: foundation stones
for lifelong happiness.

In Remembrance of You

I hold in my memory;
Your amazing smile,
The straightening of your lips,
The twinkle of your eyes,
The relaxing of your brow,
The lifting and color of your cheeks;
All of which sparks in me a wonderful
feeling of love.

I hold in my mind
The memory of your scent,
The fragrance of your body,
exuding sensuality;
Inviting touch, caress, involvement,
in connectedness of oneness.

I hold a vision of purity of speech
when communicating with you,
Your kind powerful words of wisdom,
clarity of thought,
Strength of commitment,
Demonstrating integrity, and assurance;
to honesty and certainty at all times.

I will forever hold
You in my thoughts,
For the time we spent together;
The life we shared,
The good times we had,
The challenges we faced
The victories we won,
The tears we shed,
And most of all,
The laughter and joys we shared.

What is Man?

The ancient Psalmist raised the question, (Psalm 8: 4)
"What is man that you are mindful of him?"
His question is perennial, ever present to
everyone.
Through the ages, this question is revisited
Time and again By theologians,
philosophers, teachers,
psychologists, sociologist, and psychiatrists
In an effort to come to consensus.

The question when simply put is this:
What is humanity at the core of its being?
What makes the species
different from other mammals?
Is it the ability to stand and walk upright?
Is it the power of speech and communication?
Is it the mind that causes thinking, planning,
reasoning, rationalizing and inventing?
Or, is it his spirit which enables
Co-operation, harmonization,
memorization of information?
One wonders if it is his faith,
the power of belief in what is not
Visible to the naked eye but
altogether possible?

Some conclude that man is essentially
good at the core, for he carries
the image and impress of God
his creator.
Others say that he is evil at the core
of his being; for he had lost that image
and impress of God at the Fall.
I say that there's some evil in every good man
and some good in every evil man.

Some others posit that the good in man
comes from his innate nature,
while his evil is from the nurture
imbibed from the community.

The investigation is never ending,
the inquiry will continue, but maybe not for you.
What matters in the meantime, is this:
"Know Yourself!"
Find a context for who you are at your core,
And be true to that self-awareness
and understanding in order to
actualize your greatest potential.

What Man Needs?

Some teachers and philosophers posit
That all man needs is Faith, Hope and Love.
I agree with that, but man is in need of more,
I say, man needs much more than that.

Man needs fortitude, honesty and loyalty;
Man also needs a future, integrity, and a legal system
to protect the rights of honor.
Man needs friends, health, and lodging to be human.

Man needs fellowship, to give hospitality
so that he may have longevity on the earth.
Man needs a fraternity for association
work and honor of being.

Man needs goals to reach for with morality of soul,
And he needs literature to reflect upon
present and past cultures.
Man needs funds and fire,
language and laughter,
high values to practice
and possibly a hell to remind him that
there is a heaven to gain.
That's my view of what man needs.

The Vicissitudes of Life

When life hands you a lemon,
As sometimes life does,
don't cry, don't deny
its possibilities.
You have options for its use,
with a little imagination,
ingenuity, pride and experiment;
you'll bring out its fragrance and power
in new ways.

When life lands you
on your bottom,
as is often the case;
don't just sit there
and whine and pine,
moaning and groaning,
complaining and explaining,
that you can't do anything better.
Get up! Rise up!
Take up your bed!
Get out of the shed
and shadow – and live.

When you are turned around
by life's struggles,
as often happens,
fight back with every ounce of energy
you possess in order to overcome.
Assisted by the power
that comes not from within you
but from a father God who loves you;
know that the impossible can be turned
around in His hands.

When the road of life is too easy
for you, and this seldom happens,
Enjoy its calm and precious moments.
But watch out,
plan for the change of winds,
prepare for the storms,
raging seas of disappointments,
Chaos and confusion
that are on their way to you;
Hold strong to your faith that
in the end,
all things will be well.

My Wish for You

Fountains of love,
Rivers of flowing pleasure,
Excellent health,
Peak performance and satisfaction
in your vocation;
All these I wish you in 2020.

May the abundant God
watch over you,
Guide your thoughts and steps,
Influence your decisions,
Shine the light of truth upon you;
All these I wish for you this year.

Protection from danger,
Prosperity for you and your household,
Peace and tranquility in your home,
Success in all you do;
All these I wish for you this year.

Thanksgiving

I give thanks for food and farmers who grow them,
For fowl, fish, and friends we enjoy together,
For fruits and nuts that nourishes the body
For all things edible and drinkable,
We give thanks!

For our means of transport and network of roads,
For textile and clothing, furnishing and toys;
For police and military; machinery of every sort,
For God's imparted wisdom to us in the use of them,
We give thanks!

For institutions of care, hospitals and hospices,
Doctors, nurses, and medical technicians' who care for us
in our time of need for healing and recovery;
For correctional facilities, law, courts and judges,
We give thanks!

For synagogues, temples, churches and worship,
Schools, colleges and other institutions of learning,
For children genius, normal and disabled;
For their contribution of changing home and society,
We give thanks!

For music, art, photography, world news and technology,
that makes the world a global village,
For recycling of waste and waste management
technicians, who labor for our better health and sanitation,
We give thanks!

For guardian angels visible and invisible;
Ancestral spirits in the heavens watching over us,
Encouraging, cajoling, pushing us toward the light,
and right living in harmony with self, neighbor
and the world, We give thanks!

For courage, love, contentment, patience,
tolerance and protection,
Work and leisure, time and space,
Seasons of nature and life;
Philanthropists' and charities,
Grace and goodness,
Gratitude and thanks,
For our vulnerability,
And our invincibility,
and accomplishments;
We thank You, Great God and King.

A Simple Solution to a Thorny Problem

Shopping plastic bags is a
fundamentally cheap and
advantageous method for
businesses to have their logo
advertisement not only
in your hand but in your home.

How then can the problem of
disposal of plastic bags
be accomplished in a safe
and environmentally safe way?
I propose the following simple
solution to the problem.

When I was just a lad
accompanying my mother
to the grocery store on a
Saturday afternoon;
we went with a cotton sack
made from flour bag cur in
two with a tie string sown into the top.

More affluent shoppers came
with wicker baskets and
a tea towel to cover it
for privacy.
These were ideal means to
carry one's shopping home.

Other stores would wrap
your purchases of
clothing, medicine, or
household goods in
plain wrapping paper
which was placed in your receptacle.

Today, instead of going to the
store desiring to have a plastic
bag to carry your shopping;
carry a basket, carry a homemade
sack, or use a pillowcase with a string
to tie the top.
Very environmentally friendly.

The Perils of the Ancient Farmer

The backbone of ancient farming in the Second Temple period was the animal. A healthy robust animal – ox, cow, or donkey, was the key to abundant and successful planting season.

The first peril then, is a weak, mediocre unhealthy and cantankerous animal. It was difficult to maneuver in the field, sometimes starved of enough food to enable control after which insufficient manure was produced for fertilization. Another peril was that of inconsistent weather patterns. There were times when the early rains came late, and the latter rains never came in appropriate amounts to mature the crops. Too much rain when the seeds are planted, washes away the seeds. Most times, a farmer may not have seeds for a second planting and must take a loan of seeds from another provider at a high interest rate. He may even have to sell a child to do it. Pesky insects like locust sometimes destroy the crop just before reaping. There were no deterrents against such destruction and farmers trusted their crops and placed their faith into the hands of YHWH for protection against such obliteration.

Taxation and banditry also were problematic for the ancient farmer. In times of famine, bandits would raid farms for their own survival. Taxation from colonial overlords were quite high as well as votive taxation to the temple priesthood. Farming then was a difficult undertaking, it was laborious for the entire family due in part to lack of hired laborers. A bad

year would leave many small farmers broke and for survival, would lose their land and become tenant farmers instead. Today's American farmer does not have the same concerns of their ancient counterparts. They have much more land, irrigation system, mechanized instruments, as well as efficient employees to take care of the crops.
Crops are now varied and abundant due to pesticides and artificial fertilizers, so that there is overproduction and destruction by necessity.

Lines and Voices

Above the line,
Above the voice,
Above the words,
Even above the law;
is the joy,
the craftiness,
the ecstasy of the
powerful few.
Below the line,
Below the voice,
Below the words,
Even below the law;
is the horror,
the pain,
the anguish,
the desperation,
and suffering
of the masses.
The masses cry for hope's liberation,
they cry for justice,
they cry for compassion,
in their degradation.
Yet, such cries go
unheard,

unrecognized,
un-responded to
by those who's
words are above the line
in their craftiness,
their ecstasy,
their joy.
But the masses
are relentlessly
fearless,
resilient and
uncompromising
in their efforts to eradicate
the bias,
the injustice,
the social stigma
and cruelty
of oppression.
In the end,
the weak,
single voice
united
with other weak
single voices,
grow into
an audible
and perceptible
song.
With strength that
breaks rocks,
Pillars of society;
bring low

The mighty,
The powerful,
The unjust,
ending their joy,
ecstasy,
and craftiness.

Spring into Easter

Spring into Easter with hope,
Hope of new life in Christ,
"*Christ is the way, to truth, and to life,* (John 14: 6)
Life without end is only found in Him.

Spring into Easter with great love,
Love for your neighbor and God,
God is love, and the one who is united
with God lives in love.

Spring into Easter with faith,
Faith that saves through the grace of Christ,
Christ's faith in God liberates the fallen,
Fallen are made justified by faith.

Spring into Easter with celebration,
Celebrate your faith, hope and love in Christ,
Christ within gives rise to joy,
Joy that is unspeakable and full of glory.

Spring into Easter with giving,
Giving your time, resources and efforts
To your community,
Community visibility glorifies the God of peace.

Falsehoods

Falsehoods are stock in trade
for many professions,
they are propagandistic tools
in an arsenal used for destruction.
They are applied to real issues
of great importance to the general public
with intent to mislead a nation, an
institution, a company or an individual.

Some will swallow the falsehood like
a fish swallows the bait and get hooked.
Others will be skeptical of what they hear
and raise questions as they assess
the inconsistencies.
Yet, the falsehood will take root
over time to influence the culture.
The objectives of falsehoods are varied,
to deceive, to defame, to destroy
a person's reputation, or to
destroy confidence in the
effectiveness of social, political or
educational programs.
Conspiracy theorists now boldly peddle
their falsehoods publicly in order
to plant doubt and create conflict
in the society.

Birds

There is a bird on the ground
pecking for worms,
there are birds on a high-tension wire
singing their song;
birds in a tree chirping merrily;
all through the day,
they do this cheerfully.

Birds are carefree
and sometimes silly,
other times wise in
avoiding menace;
high up in the sky or diving
deep in the oceans blue,
as you will see the penguins do.

Birds are like us
in several ways,
we live in homes
They live in nests,
and we build them aviaries;
our names are different
theirs's are too;
for example,
the Cuckoo and the Tinamou.

Many birds are good for food
like chicken, duck, turkey,
goose, and grouse.
Others are raptors or birds of prey,
like the falcon, caracara and hawk,
while some others are scavengers,
like the vultures and condors –
cleaning up the environment.

Make a bird happy today
by providing a bird feeder and water too;
For feeding and bathing in a
convenient place of your garden,
so that you will enjoy the benefits
of their music each day.

The Church House

The church house represents
the aspirational efforts of a
community to center
its spiritual life in worship,
Education, charity and faith.

In many communities,
the people pull together,
work tirelessly hard together,
raise the required sums of money,
to build and beautify that central space.

With the growth of cities
over time, generous benefactors
contribute to the efforts
to transform the tiny entity
into a magnificent cathedral.

Church houses like synagogues,
mosques and temples
are open daily for prayer
And the taking of confession, give
Alms to the poor and educate
the community's children.

Like the sin-eater of another ancient
culture, the church house stands
to absolve the sinner,
fulfilling its mission to the nation,
offering hopes of regeneration.

In recent times it becomes
a soft target of hate, violence,
and retribution; cutting down the holy
and innocent,
and burning of it down to the ground.

But like the sphinx it
rises, resurrects, springs back
to life; stands tall and defiant;
its bells ringing, calling all
to life, liberty, charity, faith and all.

Before You Pass On

Before you pass on,
you ought to know,
that through your caring
and devotion to me,
your life was worth the living.

Before you approach your maker,
it would be wise to cleanse your soul;
for He offers salvation freely,
to those who shall enter
the gates of pearl.

Before you close your eyes in death,
Be sure your conscience is without regret;
Your heart is pure, your mind at peace;
Ready as a dove for release.

Before you vacate your house of clay,
Allowing your spirit to fly freely away;
Be assured you'll never die,
In your new home in the by and by.

Before I go on to glory or
be laid out in a vegetative state;
I must be sure that my spirit house
is in order, to take its journey up on high.

Emotions

Love and hate are
standing at your gate;
hoping you will let them into
your heart to become
a part of your life.

Hope and fear,
please be aware
that fear leads to despair;
then despair leads directly
to destruction.

Truth and deception,
not in the least
new revelation;
truth will win,
and deception
will be confined to the bin.

Courage and cowardice,
will cause you
to sit down or stand
up in a crisis;
to defend the right, truth, justice,
honor and love.

Spirit, body and soul,
make the personality whole
With love not hate;
With hope not fear,
With truth not deception,
With courage not cowardice,
When the gate of the hear is opened
to honor.

For the High School Graduate

A crowning moment
has come in your life
in graduating from high school.
Now, you are on your way
to loftier challenges of life.
Congratulations!

Your future looks bright,
your character seems strong,
to continue your pursuits of
higher education, or enter
your chosen vocation.
Congratulations!

We wish you joy and peace,
courage and insight to
honestly compete;
guided by your faith in God
to make you succeed.
Congratulations!

Our hope is for you
all the days of your life
to serve Him and the

Community, genuinely;
Combined with holy living and
A true conscience.
Congratulations!

Meditations

In my meditative
half hour,
I focus on the lotus
flower,
its texture,
its color,
its power to refresh
the heart and soul.

Sometimes too
I think of you,
pondering what
will I do
if I were to suddenly lose you?
Hoping desperately
for clarity,
when I cogitate
on our bonding together.

In those sacred
moments of time,
my simple mind
is transported to
the Divine,

enabling me to
see clearly,
the hour of
my victory.

Which Move?

Move on – do not stand in the same physical,
mental or educational place for too
long. Standing there is akin to
Stagnation.

Move out – of fear, hesitation and doubt. Move
out of morbidity, stupidity, and
ignorance that will destroy your
creativity.

Move in – most quietly and unreservedly into the
lives of others, in love, faith, service in
order to fulfill your higher purpose here
on earth. Move in also to new
priorities, desires, and new vistas of
hope. Move into grace and strength to
do what is right.

Move back – to the traditions and practices of
your childhood, which, to this point,
stood you in grand favor of the elders.

Move forward – absorb the new technology, the
new social mood of society
without giving up your morality
or integrity.

Move over – into the slower lane whenever
Possible. Sometimes, we wait for circumstances to change our lane in order to give way to other's faster living.

Move up – to Christ, make Him number one in
your life. Stand for righteousness,
truth, honesty and justice.

Move down – from arrogance, pride, self-
aggrandizement, and abuse of
personal or public power entrusted
to you by the electorate.

For All Mothers

For all mothers, single
or married, with or
without children,
you have been strong
when all others were weak;
wise during other's foolishness,
calm in chaos,
feisty, protective, caring,
kind and thoughtful.
That's the reason why
this day is set aside
in honor of you.

For all mothers, young
or old, employed
or not, you are the keepers
of the flame of nurture,
the source of life,
like mother earth.
Non can doubt your
commitment in friendship,
hospitality or generosity.
That's the reason why
this day is set aside
in honor of you.

For all mothers, violated,
rejected, humiliated,
frustrated or have rights denied.
Through inspiration, tenacity,
Alacrity and persistence,
you prevail over harassment,
deprivation, calamity and crime
committed against you.
You stood your ground
When others run or give in.
That's the reason why
this day is set aside
in honor of you.

For all mothers, humble,
subtle, credible,
outrageously cunning,
when you want to,
capable, courageous, fashionable
and motivated.
Who can stand in your way?
No man or mountain,
no river of troubles.
That's the reason why
this day is set aside
in honor of you.

For all mothers, Judeo-Christian,
Hindu, Muslim, Sikh or
No religious affiliation.
Your purpose in life
Is to raise up and
Strengthen others,

educate, motivate, cogitate
on values much higher
than yourselves.
That's the reason why
this day is set aside
in honor of you.

The Movements of Music

When God Created
motion on the land, in the sea,
and in the air, He created music.

Land animals, sea creatures,
and birds of the air are also
vested with quality sounds of music.

Like the songbirds in my garden,
So also, is the laughter of my children
In my home; sweet, melodious, angelic music.

Jubal (Gen. 14: 19-22) was the first inventor
of pipes and string instruments;
The progenitor of the guitar and pipe organ.

Music is made up of
Only seven notes from A-G;
On these major and minor scales are built.

The magic of music lies
in its movements from high
to low notes and back again
in all compositions.

The effectiveness of music
is its power to create emotional
response in the musician and the listener,
no matter the mood.

Music has the power to transport
you to heights of ecstasy,
change your disposition, even drives
you into a frenzy.

One must be exposed
to all genres of music in
order to be cultured.

Sacred music is good in its place,
Sentimental old and new is good in its place,
Classical instrumentals
are good in their place.

Listen to Latin American sounds!
Listen to Afro-Caribbean sounds!
Listen to Asian-Pacific Sounds!
Listen to Euro sounds!

Each will educate, facilitate
reflection and moves you
with its movements
to heights of joy.

If Only

If only all citizens of this great and marvelous country, had the same degree of desire for its prosperity and influence in the world, there is nothing at all that would stop it being the desired utopia.

If only the one percent gives back one percent of their earnings each year to the ninety-nine percent of those who are destitute homeless, no one would be a vagrant on our streets.

If only the excess of farm produce become available to food deserts in our world, then there would not be hungry starving children breaking down our immigration doors to enter here.

If only our commercial institutions would pay a fair wage to workers, then there will be no need for parents to work two and three jobs to support their lonely children.

If only all kinds of work were mandated reasonable daylight working hours, then parents would spend quality time with children; eliminating crime from this land.

If only politicians had a moral compass to direct their decision away from their personal gains, then our infrastructure, education, and social programs would be in great shape.

If only health care was a civil right and not a privilege as is the case, then we would have a healthier population contributing to the utopia America could be.

If only guns were treated as a privilege rather than a right, then ninety percent black men would live to see their third and fourth generation, rather than dying early from gun violence.

If only you could meet me as a friend day or night on the street as was our custom in former times, then fear and hatred would be banished from our minds irrespective of our color or class or creed. If only! If only! If only!...

The Voice

The voice first spoke before the beginning of time
calling into existence the light, the land, the sea,
the beasts of the field and the vegetation for
covering the earth. Then the Voice created humans.

Humans from its inception, could
hear and obey the Voice. The Voice then was strange,
mysterious, compelling and demanding a response, as in,
"Adam, where are you?" And Adam responded, "Here I am."

The voice came to every person, directing, encouraging, informing
the individual on the path of life for successful living in harmony
with others. It worked for a time, then humans began
losing the ability to hear and positively respond to the Voice.

Meanwhile, humanity formed enclaves called societies;
Pooling their wisdom and resources for survival. Not long
after, they began to envy, domineering and eventually
enslaving those of less influence in their midst.

Yet, the Voice kept on speaking, calling, even cajoling like a concerned
parent with a wayward child. Very few had the power to hear and
obey the Voice which directed them to speak to their communities.

Irrespective of prophets and priests trying with all their power to bring the wayward back to the voice; they were ignored at times, persecuted at times, even killed for responding to the voice in their midst.

Finally, the Voice took on the form of man. He came with a perfect solution to the problem of disregard for the Voice. He began by teaching the people how to listen and respond to the Voice in their midst.

Some did respond positively while others hated him with a passion and planned His execution. On a dark stormy night, He was kidnaped and tried both by the religious And political bodies of the time. They sentenced Him to death by crucifixion.

Those who understood the Voice in human form buried him. After three days, He came back to life. He commissioned His hearers to go to every corner of the world with a message of love and forgiveness.

Those who respond to the message experience the presence of God, the love of Christ and the guidance of the Holy Spirit in their lives. They experienced peace and comfort in tribulation and assured of being in the presence of the Voice in death.

The Woman in the Window

This was 1962, when black men
Were conscripted to fight in the
Viet Nam war. John, who had
Completed his ninety-day training,
Was called up to go five months
After his training.

His lover looked at him intensely
with bright brown hopeful eyes;
with love in her face, and those eyes
told her story of fear, apprehension,
longing, and prayers for his safety
on this six-month tour of engagement.

He kissed her goodbye at the
Bottom of the apartment stairs.
She made a promise to stand in
The window that faced the street.
It was there she waved goodbye to him
as he joined the others in the back of the truck.

That truck drove them to the processing
center on the military base in Atlanta, Georgia.
From there, the flew to another base in Los Angelis, California
where they spent two additional days of briefing.

To John, the information seems more like brainwashing than useful. He made this known to her in his letter written in Los Angelis and arrived at her home five days later. She read it repeatedly to make sure she understood where he would be in this initial assignment.

Day by day, for a few hours in the evening she stood in the window as if practicing her welcome back greeting. She stood there – hoping, desiring to see his frame coming down the road toward her. But it was only three weeks ago he left, and she knew his tour of duty was six months.

She received another letter four weeks-in his leaving and was revived emotionally when she learned that he was not yet engaged in active combat. She sat at her dinner table and responded immediately to the letter sharing her innermost affection for him.

Three months passed without a return letter to her. She went and visited his parents and the recruiting office to find our if they had heard any word from John. "Negative!" was the answer she received from both enquiries. On her return home that evening, she stood longer In the window pondering.

She stood more steadfastly at her post by the window as three more months passed without a word as to John's whereabouts. Her more than average weight became wasted due to lack of sleep and poor diet. Some called her stupid, others say she was crazy, yet, she was unphased.

Two more years had passed with no Word from or about John. During that time, eligible bachelors saw her in the window and tried to woo her into a new relationship but without success. She had pledged to John she would wait for him even if it was for a lifetime.

Ten years had passed since John left for the
Viet Nam war and never came back. She began wearing
mourning clothes whenever she went out. Ten years his
lover stood in the window with expectation of his return.
Ten years of longing for John who never returned.

She had a theory that he was not killed
in battle but may have took off one night – AWOL!
He was not a violent man and his quiet disposition did not
suite him well to fight for a cause against a people based
on the reasons provided by the administration.

She continued her watch, thinking that he will find his way
home in due time. She murmured under her breath, "My
love can wait, no matter how hard it becomes, I will stand
here in the window and he will seem me on his arrival."

Alphabetical Index

1. Abiding Grace   35
2. Above or Below?   94
3. A Christmas Wish   91
4. A Simple Solution to a Thorny Problem   125
5. Before the end Comes   66
6. Before You Pass On   138
7. Birds   134
8. Blessed are the Poor   59
9. Butterfly and Rose   8
10. Can You See?   103
11. Celebrate Life   102
12. Crisis of Conscience   71
13. Daisy-Mae Millin   79
14. Death Row's Death   75
15. Did You Know?   69
16. Divisions   83
17. Does God Really Love?   49
18. Earth   20
19. Emotions   139
20. Equilibrium   85
21. Eulogy for Indonesia   88
22. Falsehoods   133
23. Fire   110
24. For All Mothers   147
25. For Janice   76
26. For the Children   73

27. For the High School Graduate   141
28. Freedom   104
29. Friends for Life   81
30. Fruits   21
31. Hallelujah!   90
32. Hands   53
33. If Only   152
34. I'm Not Forgotten   96
35. In Remembrance of You   115
36. Instructions   18
37. Judgment Day   93
38. Justice   12
39. Life's Fountain   68
40. Lines and Voices   129
41. Loving You   62
42. Marcelle J. Williams   77
43. May I Remind You?   67
44. Meditations   143
45. Money   60
46. My Alphabet of Me   39
47. My Wish for You   122
48. Nature   7
49. No Chains!   52
50. Now is the Time   87
51. Open your Eyes! Open Your Heart!   100
52. Out of my Heart   47
53. Philosophy of Love   29
54. Reparations for Me   45
55. Reproduction   55
56. Seaward Bound   10
57. Soul to Soul   19
58. Spirits for Bodies   33
59. Spring into Easter   132
60. Technology   22
61. Thanksgiving   123

62. The 35th Miami-Dade Book Fair   108
63. The Art of the Artists   98
64. The Bible   14
65. The Church House   136
66. The Conflict   106
67. The Cost of Courage   15
68. The Doctors   57
69. The Movements of Music   150
70. The Offerings   65
71. The Perils of the Ancient Farmer   127
72. The Preacher   54
73. The Tree   24
74. The Vicissitudes of Life   120
75. The Voice   154
76. The Wedding Song   13
77. The Woman in the Window   156
78. Time's End   31
79. To whom do you Pray?   64
80. Using Time Wisely   63
81. We follow in the footsteps of our Foreparents and Elders   27
82. Welcome Boy! Welcome Girl! Welcome!   41
83. What are People Like?   25
84. What a World!   16
85. What is Man?   117
86. What Man Needs?   119
87. What Shall I Bequeath my Child?   113
88. What to do in Order to Love Your Neighbor?   111
89. When?   37
90. Which Move?   145
91. Will God Come Again to Earth?   43

Biography

Answsorth Hervan Mackenzie Moitt w as born on January 18th, 1952, on the small but exquisitely beautiful island of Antigua in the West Indies. He has a strong character and sturdy in determination; thinks strategically; is self-motivated, with superb integrity. He is the seventh of ten children born to his mother and the twelfth of his father's sixteen. Both worked to support growing families.

He has had an international education: earned a diploma in Theology at West Indies Theological College, Port-of-Spain, Trinidad; a Master of Divinity and Master of Arts in Biblical Studies respectively at School of Theology, Anderson University, Anderson, Indiana; Associate of Arts in Education at Miami-Dade College, Miami, Florida; Bachelor of Science in Elementary Education and Master of Science in Reading Education respectively from Barry University, Miami Shores, Florida.

Answsorth Married Janice Browne in 1977 and became parents of Pernelle Nathaniel, also Antiguan born.

Answsorth was ordained in 1990 and served as pastor of Zion Church of God, Antigua, from 1987-1990. He and his family answered the call to serve the Tottenham Community Church of God in London, England, 1995-2001. On completion of ministry there, the family returned to Miami, Florida, 2002, where he planted and pastored the now closed Homestead Community Church of God from 2005-2016. He taught in the Miami-Dade School system for over ten years at various elementary, middle and high schools in Homestead.

Answorth is a lover of good humor and comedy. In music, beside classic gospel, he cherishes classic oratorios such as the Handel Messiah, Elijah and Joseph; as well as the West Indian expressions of the steel band, Reggae and Calypso. For Reggae and Calypso songs, his preferences are those with lyrics of social commentary that helps to awaken and strengthen consciousness of equity and justice within the community. One might even go to the length of saying that the singers of such lyrics are our modern-day prophets. In film, he likes epics/historical drama, action, adventure, and science fiction.

He does not see himself as perfect by any stretch of the imagination, but rather being perfected each day by Christ's empowerment, love and grace.

www.ingramcontent.com/pod-product-compliance
Lightning Source LLC
Chambersburg PA
CBHW020123130526
44591CB00032B/399